BULL HEART

*A personal and poetic journey
through the process of divorce ...*

BRIAN J. MUELLER

DIGITAL ALPHABET BOOKS

www.DigitalAlphabet.com

Bull heart: a personal and poetic journey through the process of divorce... / Brian J. Mueller.—First edition.
Mueller, Brian J., 1973-
ISBN: 978-0996812023 (trade paperback)

1. Poetry

First Edition: October 2015

I don't think I was a whole person until my heart was destroyed.

—Marc Maron, host WTF Podcast

To God who loves everyone and everything without fail,
and for all those who strive to do the same (albeit imperfectly).

CONTENTS

INTRODUCTION

Thank you for picking up this book. I take great pleasure in sharing my thoughts and feelings through writing and other creative endeavors. In the case of these poems I am humbled by the sadness and the spirit that set them loose. It was not my intention to write a book of poetry as I mourned the end of my marriage. This is simply how my emotions poured out. Regardless, I hope in my words you'll find a human resonance that affirms life and our connectedness, even through the pain and the suffering.

It may be hard to believe the end of a marriage that has been failing for some time can come as a surprise to anyone. Yet when my wife made her decision, I was still busily working on myself and on our marriage. Then she left me with no choice in the matter, and I had to let go.

Like a concussion grenade, the impact of divorce left me stunned and disoriented. I was overcome with grief, living away from my home, and burdened by responsibilities. After a couple of weeks the reality and permanence of my personal tragedy came into focus. At that moment I was completely devastated.

In the beginning there was little I could do but get through the day. I was faced with very practical decisions and tasks. I did the best I could on all fronts and peaceably said goodbye to my wife and the life I had known for several years. I then limped through the holiday season, after which I moved back to my hometown. It was then that the deeper healing began.

Accepting the end of my marriage was a profound step for me towards letting my life fall apart. For several years I had been questioning my path while working honestly and earnestly toward change. Little did I know the change I anticipated would be so overwhelming.

There was precious little to salvage from my marriage. I was drained physically and emotionally. It seemed the best possible outcome was for the old me to die, and so I stood in the road and let the grief overtake me.

These selected poems chronicle my journey through grief and despair to the point at which I am again standing on my own two feet. Today I am humbled, though in some ways stronger and more deeply connected with my life. I have not arrived anywhere nor am I on my own. Throughout this period of time I have reached out and accepted the support of a great many people who have taken their own voyage through pain and tragedy.

There are so many sources of profound experience and wisdom in the world it is impossible to list everyone and everything upon which I have come to rely heavily in my continued efforts towards growth and renewal. Nonetheless, I hope I can add to this bounty and inspire others as they struggle through divorce or any of the tremendous challenges life presents.

Brian
March 18, 2014

SECTION 1

Midway through life's journey, I awoke to find myself in a dark wood.

—DANTE ALIGHIERI, *THE DIVINE COMEDY*, OPENING STANZA

LAKE PONTCHARTRAIN

I come to your shores,
my back to the city,
to ground myself.

I, who am drawn to the desert
stand here scanning your waters.

In the distance the clouds gather,
your waves swell.
I watch the storm
pass right through you.

MY TESTAMENT

I did the best I could.
I remained present.
I was faithful.
I did the work of describing my feelings.
I altered my expectations.
I kept my good intentions of causing no harm.
And most importantly,
I never stopped loving her.

I recognized
how overwhelmed she was,
not privy to my thoughts and intentions
even as I offered them.

I guess it appeared to her as if
I was being destroyed from the inside out,
spirit devouring the flesh.
For me it was a torturous baptism into awakening,
an excruciating initiation into staggering transformation.

The demons that practice madness
are mostly gone now,
I remain, more or less the same in form,
entirely different in spirit.

Loss redeemed me.
When I turn back in anger
I see a marriage smoldering in ruin.
The smoke made more pungent
by her infidelity and greed.

I turn away and back again in forgiveness.
I see a good and honest man
altered by life and by God's love.

It will never be right.
This deeper understanding brings me
into union with all life.
Now heading in the direction of the light,
I am given the grace to let go.

CHRISTMAS

My wife decided more than a year ago
she didn't want to be married.

Too hard.

Yeah.

So was divorce.

Last year I wandered around
like a shell-shocked soldier
clutching my heart in my hand.

It didn't stop beating
but turned a deeper shade of red.

This year I'm putting it in a box.
gonna wrap it
and re-gift it to myself.

GIFT LIFE

I knew my life was good,
but I wanted to know I earned it,
so I went to school to learn it,
took a job to work it,
found some books to read it,
gave it away to receive it,
married in order to love it,
lost it.

Until…

I fell
naked
into it.

LIKE A BULL

I stand alone in the shade;
the world I observe is chaotic.
Like a bull I wait patiently,
suppressing all of my urges.

Some can see it; others cannot.
Breathe in, breathe out.
The breeze picks up.
I feel a surge.
My pulse quickens, I isolate a beautiful woman in all that noise.
Her pants are so tight they reveal the contours of her lower half.
My yearning makes me grimace.
Life, not this woman, is beckoning me.

The stillness of this spot is so seductive
I want to remain here forever.
There is no pain from confrontation.
There is no pleasure from connection.
I must reach toward a greater love,
and risk falling into serenity.

TRANSFORMATION

True healing is transformation.
It is a gift primarily given by self.

Can it be earned?
It is a grace arising from life's journey.

Can it be refused?
It will call again undaunted.

How will I know I am transformed?
You will feel it. Others will see it.

Are we talking about death?
Merely acceptance of it.

So I must be willing to die?
Again and again.

SECTION 2

Sometimes, in a summer morning, having taken my accustomed bath, I sat in my sunny doorway from sunrise till noon, rapt in a revery, amidst the pines and hickories and sumachs, in undisturbed solitude and stillness, while the birds sing around or flitted noiseless through the house, until by the sun falling in at my west window, or the noise of some traveller's wagon on the distant highway, I was reminded of the lapse of time. I grew in those seasons like corn in the night, and they were far better than any work of the hands would have been.

—HENRY DAVID THOREAU, *WALDEN*, CHAPTER 4: SOUNDS

MY DIVORCE STORY (THE JOURNEY)

I stand alone amidst the corpses of my memories and dreams.
There will be no reconciliation of what happened here.
I steel myself for a journey.
My heart again beating;
where is my mind?

GRIEF

Sadness lurks in the dark hours of early morning
until I push it away.

Every day begins this way,
a little more, a little less.
As the sun rises I start to forget;
then in the pile of mail I see your name,
and like Sisyphus I labor to find peace.

EL DIVORCIADO

Am I breathing?
A shallow breath
stumbling in darkness.
Flash! A blinding light.

Days drip by,
indistinguishable.
My heart burns.
Why am I cold?

Alone in this desert,
dry, only dust,
not even a mirage;
am I a ghost?

A soul gone missing,
shells on a beach,
merry-go-round,
littered side-street.

Surrender your badge.
Bleed no more.
A bee stings,
a snowflake melts.

Soft wet lips,
steady, rhythm drum
¡Vaya con dios!
Life marches on.

I'M NOT IMPOSSIBLE

I don't know what I thought would happen.
I'm tired of being tired and unsatisfied.
Nothing will ever satisfy me;
I know this because she told me.

There's a place in each of us, deeper than any ocean,
where the undertow is so powerful
we are all moved beneath the surface.

My heart is full.
I love and am loved,
this I never forget.

Still I'm searching for the kind of fullness
a man my age knows
comes only from within.

I got the message clearly:
If life was easy everyone would live in bliss.
Still, how much is grace and how much action?

THOUGHT

I shape my world with thought.

If I had never uttered
the word divorce
in the presence of my ex-wife
she would not be thus.

It makes me wonder just a little bit about
the vindictive human spirit.

COLDEST MORNINGS

The coldest mornings are the clearest,
the light brightest on the horizon.
A friend tells me this crisp weather makes her feel alive.
Me too, if only to keep warm.

My pain arrives at the appointed hour
on these chilly mornings.
Only one other person possibly shares it,
but I don't know her any longer.

These feelings are too heavy for me alone.
So I sit on this bitter cold morning and add them to my poem,
or I go to a meeting and insert them into my conversation.
As I grow in strength and wisdom, divine alchemy makes them love.

SAY A PRAYER FOR ME

Words are oft times my greatest comfort.
So please say a prayer for me,
that I may loose my grip on this diving bell
and float back to the surface
like thousands of tiny bubbles,
that I may breathe the air no matter how cold and dry,
living among others,
accosted by vandals, pick-pocketed
as we move from one glorious place to another.

FIRE

I carry an ember,
hold it out,
coax the flame with my breath.

In the light I see many faces
similar to my own,
each carrying a stick
they wish to ignite.

Where once I stood guard
now I stand back.
Make your own fires.
Just know this is not the truth.
It is a mere spark
of the eternal flame.

FALLING APART

Am I difficult to live with?

This heart is full of love,
my intentions true.
So what drove me crazy?
Could it have been my loneliness?
A marriage with too little for me,
requiring every ounce of my being,
an inevitable collapse?

Darkness is an unholy beast,
sustained and nourished
by feeding upon itself.

She would collapse into bed in the early morning;
I had been awake for hours.

These guys bought us dinner and drinks.
My silence surprises me.

JANUARY

I wake up to the cold
with a cold.

My life is a gift,
even if frozen
in liminal space.

The warmth of my heart,
always in tune with spring,
holds me.

HURT

I keep my hurt contained and packaged neatly.
It's greasy and it stains.
And it stinks to high heaven,
reeking of ammonia.

I name my hurt.
I call it bloody, hot, overwhelming, hideous, debilitating, angry, desperate.
Then I put it back in its box,
tell everyone I'm above it,
that it's not important.

This is my recipe for forgiveness,
because a part of me thinks I must.
And I tell myself it takes a big heart to survive.

On my shelf is a shiny box heavy
within the proverbial polished turd.

Now is the time
to root around in it,
show it to myself and to another,
allow it to wash over me like a waterfall
until the box is empty.

FORGIVENESS

Holding the pain is like running
with a handful of water,
wetness evaporating on the pavement, or joining the soil.

Feet in the mud I stand strong against the breeze,
add compassion to my list of names,
call my tormenters to task with gratitude,
exalted by the blood gushing out of my heart.

First a vacuous silence,
then a chorus of shrieking Harpies,
next a rock speaks to me, and then a bird calls my name.
A hand reaches out for me, another and then another.
I grab fingers, hands, wrists, forearms, shoulders, torsos.
We embrace.
I am human.
I am alive.
I am forgiven.

ADRIFT

I am not alone in knowing
What it feels like to be yoked
to a partner unwilling and unable
to fully give herself to another.

Generous people share their stories with me,
their own journeys through uncertainty.

A wisdom and grace more powerful than my will
cast me far from shore;
alone I drift.

The unknown surrounds my little raft.
I fear being overwhelmed by the unpredictable current.
Then the wind whispers in my ear, "Surrender to me."
With no course to plot, I say a prayer for life.

ANNIE

I gave you all I had.

I accept your decision.
Our marriage was failing.
I failed.

The pain is humiliating.

Scars form and then recede into familiarity.

I say a prayer for your deepest well-being
and I wish you happiness, safety, and peace,
so that I may reflect on my own with gratitude.

SECTION 3

In all of nature, no storm can last forever.

—LAO TZU, *TAO TE CHING*

FIELD THEORY

Energy
surrounds me
then confounds me.

Closest as I wake
in that lucid state;
my dreams bring past into present
untangling my reality.

This energy of being,
more elusive through effort,
fills me with light,
creates the words on this page
as I dissolve into awe.

FORGIVENESS

Letting go is my grace.
It comes without toil, a breath,
an exhale.

I wake when it's still dark.
A fire truck rolls by.
Engine brakes roar, the red water dragon stops.
Then it growls off who knows where.

My breath returns.
Along with some sadness.
An opera scene opens in my mind
filled with large boulders.
A young tenor sings tales of woe
While the wind chorus,
carries them into the air.

His words will never find their intended,
and even so would be unintelligible.
Still he sings
until his breath gives out.

An exhale:
forgiveness returns.

TOWARD PAIN

Move toward the pain,
smile if you can,
laugh even.
Just do it;
you won't be sorry.
God Almighty it hurts!
White hot
dull
then sharp
suffocating
almost completely
overwhelming finally
stillness.
Is it still there?
Of course,
I can still feel it,
though a little less.
Still familiar,
I make friends with it;
we have an understanding
called serenity.

THE JOURNEY IS ME

Tears form,
and my heart turns to lead.
My departure date is approaching.
Why go?
Why indeed.
Why the rain?
Better yet, why Wall Street?

Am I not content?

There is only one true answer.
"Yes, and…"

No two trips are ever the same.
I go with an open heart, an open mind.
Though I go out into the world,
you know it,
the journey is me.

A HUMBLE LIGHT

I carry a light with me like a flare.
It's mine,
a spark of truth -
not the whole thing.
Some can see it, though I haven't shown it,
and I can see theirs.
We nod, maybe even share the warmth.
So it goes…

We nurture or neglect this tiny light
as we choose.
It grows brighter
joined with others.
I'll never forget seeing her light the first time:
unfamiliar and fragile.
Who knows what she thought of my light?
She mistook it for the truth.
I guess I wanted to believe it too,
I agreed to the lie,
smile,
wink.

Soon enough came the rain.
First slow,
then steady,
inevitably a deluge.

My flame went out.
Seeing this, she took her flame,
departed.
Mine wasn't the truth after all.

How do you live without a light?
How frightening it is,
to feel the darkness coiling around you!

Finally
I consented to die
then begged for a pardon,
said a prayer for humility.
And almost as suddenly came the light of others,
along with the love to relight my own.

OVERMATCHED

How I ever got fixated on you,
I can't say for certain.
I write the words
and I know this is bullshit.
You were just the right mixture of pretty and sweet:
the perfect cocktail.
I drank, and drank, and drank.

I got sick.
What can I say?
I wanted more.
You didn't have anything else behind the bar.
I got lousy.
I just wanted some water,
a moment of peace,
anything.
Instead you took it all away...
first the sweet drinks,
and then you to pour them.

Cold turkey wasn't my choice.

NEEDINESS

You didn't need me
but I needed more of you.
Life seemed easier for you
when you found me.
For this, I was happy.
A gift to be able to give.

So little remained to nourish me.
I turned to a higher power.
"Humility," came the response.
My proud heart balked.
You watched confused,
certain I was going to die,
'cause I told you that's how I felt.

You increased your distance,
finally stealing away.

If this is a gift,
I thank you.

GRATITUDE

Shifting my focus
back to me
ends the violence
of imposing my will
on others.

It defines control narrowly,
accepts love unconditionally,
removes judgment
as it returns me to calm.

The rhythmic thumping of my heart
marching toward exhale:
this is the ecstasy,
that the prophets wrote about.
(My beautifully imperfect life,
how is it not intended to be so?)

I belong!
We all belong!
There is only pain
when we deny our humanity,
the bond of love with all of life.

How can I feel anything but gratitude!

NEVER-ENDING JOURNEY

So much whooshin' through my head.
Like the two beautiful women,
both of 'em my age
at the party last night.
Both of 'em with somebody else.
The one folksy from rural Indiana:
she's got deep eyes and a tattoo.
Something tells me she's flirted with death.
I like her boyfriend.

The other has heard of me,
knows my nickname,
seems to like me already,
her husband legendary, blue collar,
salt of the earth, not meant for a suit.
She looks to me like a politician's wife.

I feel an empty yearning,
I want, I need, I feel
in no particular order.

I thought my salvation was a woman.
Drunk Rick asks me soberly,
"Is this your first time going through this?"
He's had more than his share.
I'm embarrassed to admit it.

Drunk Rick knows what I know.
The pain is the only real thing.
My ex has buried me.
Reality doesn't get any more stark
unless you add blood.

I'm hitting the road to let go
(some more).
It's a warm 29F.
Your life is this journey.

SPRINGFIELD

Springfield, Missouri
or thereabouts,
dawn is still a couple hours off.
I wake in my rental car,
my first night at a KOA.

It was chilly,
still not too cold.
A sleeping bag and my cap
worked well to keep me warm
on a crystal January night.

In the distance red lights flash
delineate the smokestacks of a power plant.
Every hour a train horn shatters the silence
as a two-hundred-ton diesel thunders past.
Neither can drown out the stars.

I am lonely, not alone.
This part of my journey,
at times eerily quiet,
is abundant with life, with love,
as I travel with my higher power.

FORGIVENESS (PART 2)

I hope she has forgiven me,
says an occasional prayer for my well-being.
I need this from everyone I've wronged,
no one more than myself.

What do you do when you've done the unforgiveable?
You forgive yourself.

I still sometimes wonder.
Why must I be forgiven?
The answer does not come so easily.

There is stillness after any great tragedy
a fire, a tornado, a divorce.
I had to lose what I thought most precious
to comprehend the value of my tiny life.

I held tightly to my honorable manhood,
the mythic marriage of my making.
Not even death could've saved me.
My salvation, my redemption, my forgiveness:
my insignificance.

THE RAWNESS OF A BROKEN HEART

To touch,
be touched,
to hold,
and to be held.

Just being in this world
increases my yearning.

I got the relationships I deserved:
a marriage based upon neediness,
six years that emptied my soul,
then abandoned me at my darkest hour.

The rawness of a broken heart
keeps you alive
just so it can be felt.
It keeps others away,
forcing you
to really reckon with it.

Go to war with a broken heart at your own peril.
Just let it defeat you.
When the fires subside,
when you exhale your last breath of resistance,
a calm ensues.
In this moment your heart
may again accept the seeds of love.

BELONGING

The world is enormous.
It took me less than a day on the road
to be reminded.
I glide over hills and into valleys
the highway an endless, unbroken path
of dashed lines and painted signs.
I belittle the distances
even as I catapult further into the abyss.

Three days are gone.
The road is the same.
The trucks are the same.
The diesel rumble is the same.
The stores and businesses are the same.
The food is the same.
The questions are the same.
I am the same.

The people are a little different,
otherwise, they're just like me.
They are me.
They drive like me.
Walk like me.
Eat like me.
Rely on their phones like me.
Stop at rest areas like me.

I said hello to a smoker.
He admitted driving was hard for him,
just like me.

Eating at Indian Casinos,
camping at KOA,
talkin' to whoever will talk,
livin' life closer to the present,
I see that I belong,
somewhere, anywhere, right here.

THE IMPORTANCE OF SLEEP

By day
I keep my fear
my cravings
at bay.

Fatigue,
nightfall,
and the constant tug of loneliness
prey upon my peace of mind.

Preparing for bed
it is all I can do
to keep my demons
contained.

I close my eyes
my heart trembles
as I invite the pain.
Move closer
so I can see you.

I inhale deeply
hoping to take in
the love that is God.
If I sleep
I will see my fears anew.

MY ATTENTION

My life is less
about any one thing
than it once was.

This realization comes, like so many,
in a moment of respite
alone and moving deliberately.

My mind always active and powerful.
What is noise, what is ego?
Is my awareness a curse?

I recognize big things as they are happening.
I notice seismic shifts
though it takes me time to articulate them.

How authentic is my awareness?
I once doubted it
not understanding how it connected me to my life.

I tried to turn it off and couldn't.
I sought distraction to subvert it.
I made it stronger.

Alone, a little cold and uncomfortable,
I relax into my humility with a deep breath,
at ease with my transformation.

PRECIOUS STILLNESS

Sitting in the dark
reading about death and resurrection.

I'm given pause
as I think
to my own biological imperatives,
to the women I've known desperate for a baby.
Is this really life yearning for life?
Or is it a general desire to truly be alive,
human beings in a modern world,
desperate for authenticity,
searching in all the wrong places.

My gift
to have traveled far
has brought me only inches closer to the truth.
My learning, formal and informal
are all hints, cosmic guideposts
pointing to the present moment,
the precious stillness.

Alone in the dark,
the rattling of the heater,
outside it's 18 degrees.
Inside I am warm.
I surrender to my life.

PASSAGES

What time is it?
I ask frequently,
almost immediately
as I emerge from sleep.

I am truly sorry
if I have wielded time
like a bludgeon.

The more experience I accumulate
the past comes into perspective.
And with this articulation
I fill with dread.

What happened to my youth?
Such questions seem trivial,
quaint reminders of eighteenth century enlightenment,
or that guy you sat next to at a bar.

But this is big shit,
fucking, death and infinity.
It all fits equally well
into a pint glass, or the Grand Canyon.
Redemption a bit of gravel in your shoe.

The sun and shadows
are my favorite representations of time,
the displacement of light and dark
on all manner of shapes and surfaces.
This is my life.

In this one last moment
before the next,
I add my humble reverence
to the appreciation life has for itself.

AT NIGHT

The mythic me falls apart.
The brave warrior,
the stolid intellectual,
the peaceful philosopher,
the clever wit,
the lone gun:
they all go.

When the loneliness comes,
the wide open desert darkness,
terrifies me.
With its wind and space,
the forest darkness
envelops me
with its dense branches and strange sounds.

I lock myself away,
biding my time
until morning.
I will survive.
I will survive.
I will survive,
to see the true me resurrected.

INEVITABLE DEATH

The war can be ended unilaterally.
Just call the whole thing off.
Immediately the struggle will be over,
life and death brought back together,
a soul in union with the Universe.

It feels strange
at odd hours of the night or day
to contemplate my recent death
knowing its inevitability,
the necessary step
in my own resurrection,
the revelation of my naked humanity.

Oh, how I fought it!
Along the way resenting those
from whom grace flows so easily.

I thought my love was special,
ambrosia of the gods,
my unique gift to bestow
in the tiny world where I held dominion,

Fortunately it was I
my poison killed,
and the true me
it returned to this world.

NEWLYWEDS

I see the familiar rings
on the anointed fingers,
and the more familiar patterns
of togetherness,
newness.

A window into my past,
a glimpse into your future.
Mostly it's just uncertainty,
and a little jealousy,
finally a wish
for your happiness
as it comes through growth
and an abiding love.

SECTION 4

You will either step forward into growth or backward into safety.

—ABRAHAM MASLOW

THE LOVE YOU BRING

Just as there is no virtue in suffering,
there is none in proving
the limits of someone else's love.

As suffering creates growth,
so too does the realization,
grounded in our humanity,
that love is infinite.

From time immemorial,
all living creatures,
and indeed all of life,
have known God as love.

So go bravely.
For wherever you perceive a void,
it will be filled
with the love you bring.

ABUNDANCE

Why is it so hard for me
to fully comprehend,
to internalize,
the abundance of life?

Why indeed.
I have seen it.
I have been gifted it.
I have even offered it.

I must remember this,
when pain and sorrow come calling,
displacing feelings of peace,
taking with them my sense of abundance.

SEEDS OF SAMENESS

Out on the road
there was a clarity,
a more rational being
in the moment,
my path a little straighter,
the view more distant,
existing not by thought,
alive.

In this state I came
more fully into myself.
Nudging me forward,
with my imperfect voice,
to sew the seeds of sameness.
With whomever,
with whatever,
whenever.

And when I began to long for home
I was reminded
I am home.

RIVER

There is a great deal of wisdom
a great deal of grace
flowing through the fractured rock of the canyon.

The advancing water carves the stone
reveals ever deeper layers
carries away sediment
all the while spilling out
the loves,
the losses,
and even the ordinary
of my life.

KELLY

Though love is never lost
it comes and it goes
in many ways.

Quick as a chair
pulled out from under me.
Slow as a swimming pool
after Labor Day.

It goes
sight unseen and without a sound
finally crashing in
on a cold December morning.

THE ONES TO KEEP

How do you know the ones to keep,
and the ones who will keep you?

The answer precedes the question:
one part faith,
two parts love.
It is that simple.
So long as you always keep room for pain.

EMOTIONAL SOBRIETY

My heart and mind attach this morning
to my mother's existential sadness
and my desire to eliminate it.

There are countless ways to frame my wish,
most of them burnishing a son's motives.
Still I am awake and clear.
I have grown sober through my own sorrow,
which has made me realize
I have no business meddling with feelings.

My mother's pain preceded me;
it may have even led her down the path
in which I came to be.

RELATIONSHIP MAN

There is a cultural disconnect
written in confused silences
dismissed in avoidance.

The fact that I was unhappy
that through my efforts
to examine the relationship
to understand my behavior
to change myself and to grow
to explore ever deeper levels of emotion,
my marriage ended.

What was confounding
now makes perfect sense,
but that is not my point.
I write this poem for all the men
whose desire for relationship
exceeds societal norms.

There are many women
as broken as any man
numb, hard, cold,
unable to connect to their emotions.

CORAZÓN

My heart just opened
like a dropped egg,
no witnesses, only silence.

I think it kinda funny now
how it kept doin' what it needed to
in order to keep me alive,
spilling out only grief, spreading only compassion.

BACKFIRE

I told you I loved you so often
it lost all meaning.

Three simple words,
one tiny declarative,
passionate as rhythm and a red dress,
solid as a granite boulder,
painful as the longest, most difficult day.

The *I love yous* I sent,
not always the lightest gifts,
wrapped as they were in my needs,
changed me forever as they were returned.

So I opened them for myself.

ANOTHER DEPARTURE

There is no avoiding my pain
and yet I try.
There is some consolation in knowing this
even more in the way struggling binds me
to my humanity,
to all of life.

Today I leave my home again,
saying goodbye to my parents,
wishing my friends well,
thanking all the familiar people.
I am not
I could not
without them.

Equally difficult
is to remain
fixed.
My hometown grounds me
then pushes me away
a gateway to a larger world.

I pray only
that I follow a calling,
going forth to spread and to find love,
never turning away from those who need me.

NO MATTER

The details
don't matter to me
anymore.
Old fireworks,
bursts of energy in my mind and body,
explode in strange narratives,
colorful dreams.
They are a fading light,
and then they are gone.
The sulfur smell lingers,
then is blown away.

My lifetime
a blip in the cycle.
How can anything matter more
than my belonging?

NOSTALGIA

When the days gone by
return in my dreams,
familiar faces, strong emotions,
I awaken heartbroken and a little confused.

The repetitions of these moments
are farewells,
the urging onward,
a great push from the Creator
toward the inevitable fulfillment
of my life in this Universe.

TRUTH

I don't know is a release,
an honest look in the mirror,
a way to continue creating my life.

CLICK!

Time is not a camera,
even as moments are frozen in my mind.
Click!
That rock face contains the history of one hundred million years.
Click!
My face contains the story of forty.

Samsāra:
the cycle of life,
or is it the cycle of suffering?
This morning I embrace my suffering,
welcoming thoughts about my mistakes,
mourning the losses.
Why not own them?
As if there was a choice in the matter.
As if the details really meant something.
Time is not the camera;
I am.

LIGHTEN UP

If connection
through life
through consciousness
is the rational order of the Universe,
why do I feel so disconnected?

Standing on the shoulders of ancient mystics,
Yoda said:
You must unlearn what you have learned.

(If this does not enlighten me
to take life and myself
a little less seriously,
nothing will.)

PROGRESS

As I grow older
my body offers more specific instructions.
First in subtle ways:
what not to do,
what not to eat and drink.

And of course I resist
even though I want to feel good,
to be at peace.

Joy has never come
in my resistance to anything,
especially with regard to my physical body.

Though I often resist,
I now hear my body urgently telling me
to eat and drink well,
and as I do these activities,
to listen to for more instructions
in the present moment.

NO TURNING BACK

The road leads me everywhere,
past the trees
into the desert
back to the sea.

The road well-worn but unpaved,
mile after interesting mile,
I get stuck in mud.
Or I must stop to empty gravel from my shoe.
I pass strangers,
some kind,
some carrying even more than I.

The road has no signs, no markers.
There is no sense of urgency,
no shortcut,
but plenty of roadside diversions
buzzing with activity,
tantalizing the senses,
urging me to indulge my hunger.

The road is my constant.
Though I am changed,
when I am lost, struggling to let go,
without judgment, it shows me the way
and the wind whispers, "No turning back."

UNCONDITIONAL LOVE

My heart goes out,
and I find it easier
to connect with children,
when they are around.

They are not fixed,
unable to be rigid.
Except in their momentary desires,
they remain open to the world.

To be around them fills me
with peace, with hope, with love.
Even as they demand my attention,
there is nothing I can do to resist.

I watch others relate to children.
They too are drawn in magnetically.
Yet no one can get as close to them as their mother;
they are her innermost expression of love and creativity.

Still that love exists within me,
given abundantly by my own mother.
I feel it deeply, groaning as it pushes me
ever outward toward love, toward connection.

"YES, AND..."

How glorious it is to be alive,
to feel the spirit of life moving
in all its mysterious ways,
the peaks and depths of my existence.

And how joyous it is to write.
The emotions that move my pen,
difficult though they may be,
verbs, nouns, adjectives, create serenity.

Try as I might
there is no way to subtract
only the pain from my being.
Life begins and ends with *and*.

SIMPLE GIFTS

There is so much beauty in the world
I find myself turning away,
closing my eyes,
trying to suppress my need
to possess it.

Those blue emotive eyes,
the smile of a child,
the winter sky reflecting a rainbow,
the right tool for the job,
the sweetest bite of cake.

I want to own it all,
and failing this, to simply be a part of it,
to know my own beauty,
perhaps share it in verse,
a gift offered in humility.

SURRENDER

I read the words aloud.
Two others listened,
how I came to understand God,
love, the creative genius,
my broken path to reunification,
to fall apart,
completely
(or not at all).
Resurrected with uncertainty,
yet unable to go back,
my life will never be the same
(thank God).

EMPTY

No words remain
to describe my marriage,
to parse the lessons hard earned,
to give my broken self one more lament,
yet another moment to be wronged.

I'm empty.
Those difficult feelings have moved.
They find other pain to validate
before yielding to the present moment
and on down the road.

If I ever turn back in sadness,
it is because the present demands the attention
I am unwilling to give it
while resisting the light of creation,
until I breathe in the love that surrounds me.

LOVE IMMORTAL

There is no end to love or else
the God within me should die.

I have tried to become indifferent
and cannot.
Even when pain tempts me toward hate,
it is ultimately love,
in a kaleidoscopic panoply,
through which I exhale.

WANTING TO GET BETTER

Which is to say wanting to grow,
to change,
in a new direction
advertising new destinations.

I won't get there with a wish.
A new course
requires new behaviors.

The pain of growth is real,
yet no more real
than the routine behavior
of stubborn resistance.

The way forward is paved,
well-traveled,
already within me.

GROUNDLESS

A life put on and worn
can be brutal.
Even if by all appearances it seems serene,
indoors, a tempest.

The *I* that is my ego
never wanted to let go,
never wanted to let things fall apart,
only knew the concept of self preservation,
could only measure loss.

That *I* is dead.
Remnants remain in my pain,
then float away like clouds.
I wake in groundlessness.

I feel lighter than I have
since I was a child.
And though the innocence is long gone,
tears create the mud
which covers me in forgiveness.

Even as I am born again
my senses as strong as ever,
remind me where my pain resides.
So I go deeper to the love that is my being
and connect to that in others.

FIRST LIGHT

At first light
it seems
today is about sadness,
the sudden waking
to an upset stomach,
grumbling,
arousing old pain,
picking at wounds.
But it needn't be so,
everything turning over,
melting even,
like snow becoming water,
and dripping away.

Love is not lost.
And so this day begins
with a blink,
with an exhale,
with a hug,
even with a headache.

SILENT PEOPLE

There are some feelings
akin to my pain
I cannot touch.

It frightens me to think they are too near,
though that isn't quite right.
It seems they are fading
into forgiveness as I let them go,
or that I never really knew them at all.

I have a tremendous capacity to feel.
Life gives me empathy and intuition
through which I often find myself
face to face with God.
And still I cannot see into the darkness.

There are feelings attached to people
I wish to bring closer.
Their silence is a fortress.

I step back.
Just naming pain
is like taking a drink from a fire hose.
We must drown a thousand times
before we learn to live under water.

BALLOON

My grieving has come to an end.
Words about my marriage are difficult to write.
Where despair once moved my pen,
the reservoir of pain is running dry.

From time to time dark clouds surround me,
but they bring no more than a drop or two of rain.
I embrace my pain, understand its yearnings,
as it returns me to the source of our connectedness.

I fell in love and held it
more tightly than a child to a balloon,
expecting it to carry me to new heights,
tripped, let go,
it flew away without me.

What a balloon it was!
Divinely given,
but only for a moment,
so that I might open more deeply.

DANTE DEO

Something stirred the pot this week,
a fact I hate to admit,
a conversation with a friend,
or maybe the bourbon last night.
All I know is I've stumbled backward.

Again today I woke suddenly,
a little too early.
In my dream a woman I loved
carved off a piece of her own ear,
yet it was my ear that bled, I who felt the pain.

My image of God creates me,
my love takes form in this world.

Who knew how painful it would be
to put down my shield,
how exposing those vulnerable parts within
would bring humiliation, transformation, resurrection.

The daily grind to move forward
through very little joy, mostly discomfort and pain,
an honest regimen.

When I yawn awake each morning
a groan I make
as I continue to be created.

AFTERWORD

Hello Dear Reader!

Thank you for picking up this book. My name is Brian and I am the author. It is a privilege for me to share my poetry with you. I truly hope you find my words both meaningful and resonant.

I grew up in a fairly typical family in Cincinnati, OH, and for many years I followed a predictable path through life. At school I was very fortunate to receive a liberal arts education which provided a strong grounding as my life became more challenging.

For many years I had plenty of words but little to say. Only through difficult experience has my life been spiritually enriched so that at last I hope and pray my writing contains something of substance to offer to others. It is in this spirit that I have published *Bull Heart*.

Please feel free to leave me comments @ my website: www.DigitalAlphabet.com.

ACKNOWLEDGE-MENTS

I published my first book of poetry in 2002. I never imagined more than ten years would pass before I published again. It is therefore I am very grateful for this opportunity, and even for the difficult inspiration which brought forth these poems.

To my family and friends, I want to tell you how much I appreciate your love and support. You know what these poems mean to me and to my emotional healing. And I want to offer additional thanks to everyone who provided encouragement and editorial assistance.

I also wish to offer a special word of thanks to Kate Kearns of Black Squirrel Workshop for her patient and thorough editing.

Finally, a word of gratitude to my ex-wife, for the love and experiences we once shared. Had it not been for our marriage and divorce, I may not have collapsed into the arms of God and discovered my true self. I wish you the best.

www.ingramcontent.com/pod-product-compliance
Lightning Source LLC
LaVergne TN
LVHW011213080426
835508LV00007B/767